LESSONS I LEARNED FROM MY FATHER

A Book About Child Abuse

David R. Ulrich

Does Not Wisdom Call?

ISBN: 978-0-578-27311-2

Cover illustration by Hanlin Zhang All rights reserved - used with permission.

PRINTED IN THE UNITED STATES OF AMERICA

Table of Contents

Dedication

I dedicate this book to Dr. Luis Ramirez, the understanding and compassionate psychiatrist who led me to health. After discovering how badly abused I had been by a series of "tests" he devised to see how I responded, he said he was going to build me an ego and so he did. It is a very good one. He further said no one gave me the tools to become my own person, to be my own man, to live life well; and he has taught them to me as I was ready to receive them; otherwise, I would be a man who smoked and drank too much, unhappy with life, merely a braggart and show-off, with many obsessions, addictions, and compulsive behaviors, like I was when we first met. It was only because of his inexhaustible patience and unconditional positive regard for me that I was able to heal. The fact that he is a genius did not hurt. What he saw in me at the beginning so that he was willing to go to the great lengths he has, I have no idea. But I am so very grateful to him. On two separate occasions, I would not even accept a cup of coffee from him when we first met, so untrusting was I of him; and I love coffee.

It has been a process that has taken three decades, not only because I had been so badly abused, but because I am also very head strong. A sad fact about abused people is that the rules they are made to live by, set by their abusers, are so unfair that they often have to ignore them and live by their own rules. This allows them to survive while in the presence of their abuser(s), but does not bode well for them in society, where the rules are much fairer and the punishment for not abiding by them can be as simple as non-admission into life's finer organizations and circles of emotionally healthy people. Worse still is when abuser(s) change the rules frequently so that the child is kept in constant confusion and has no recourse but to live by his own rules. This also was my experience. Even now, it hinders me when I go from one social environment to another in picking up on the nuances of the established ways of doing things, so use to doing things my own way am I. Though I well understood what my father was all about, I have often found other people's intentions and motivations toward me confusing, and therefore, by extension from my experiences with my father, threatening, though they often were not. But I only recognized this fact much too late.

A sad fact is, an abused child is made to believe he is not good enough, that he is unlovable, and that he needs to be better and more capable in all ways. It resulted in me doing things at break-neck speed, trying to become better and better, doing more and more, to catch up to my father's expectations of me. I became so task oriented that I hardly noticed other people. But rushing through life, mainly unaware of those around you does not work in any society, on any level. One person told me that I had no idea the affect I had on people. She also told me that I was harder on myself than anybody she ever knew. In my self-talk, I was constantly calling myself, "stupid," idiot,"and "dummy," so unhappy with myself and my life was I.

Among the last things Dr. Ramirez said to me was, "Now combine your psychology and your religion;" since I had been a minister for a brief time, one of the disastrous decisions I made, this one to atone for my accident which I will describe later in this book. I was very ill-suited for ministry, which fortunately quickly became evident to me, and I left ministry to pursue other lines of work. It took several years for me to take my Christianity seriously again, after he told me to, and I now enjoy a wonderful relationship with the Lord. Each time I read Scripture, which is every morning, I learn something new from it, getting fresh insights and wisdom for my life. It is the case that a person understands God according to how one's father has treated him or her. I could only view God as very punitive, a God who was watching me closely, ready to strike me at the occurrence of any and every misstep, and oh so happy to do so, as my father had been. Only the Biblical passages dealing with God's wrath spoke to me back then. Nothing of His grace and mercy, love and compassion ever entered my awareness. Back when I started therapy, I read somewhere that when one is trying to overcome the damage caused by child abuse, one should not read the Bible or think much about God. I understood why and limited my reading of the Bible at first. I have slowly come to see God in a new light, to be much like Dr. Ramirez, patient, forgiving, and kind.

Foreword

I hope you find this book easy to read. But more than being entertained, I hope you get an understanding of the devastating consequences of child abuse, as it affects its victims far beyond the actual abuse, often lasting throughout the entire course of their lives. During my therapy I read and studied what abuse does to the human mind, causing its victim to view the world and all its people as hostile and unfriendly. It turns a little child into a hypervigilant, very wary individual, watching for the next blow to be struck, the next punch to be thrown, the next criticism, accusation, or insult to be hurled in his or her direction. The person who has been abused does not expect others to be good or helpful to him, and he is wary of any act of kindness, often not knowing how to respond. It alters his or her interpretation of what others say to him, or do for him. It results in a lifetime of being suspicious of everybody. In therapy, I slowly came to realize that people's words had little meaning for me as I was hardly listening to them, instead watching for any sign that an act of violence was to suddenly be thrust upon me. When one's mind and body live in such a high state of vigilance and anxiety, it wreaks havoc within him. Due to the stress it creates, living in such a state causes physical ailments as well as mental issues. It also does not allow one to concentrate, to study, or make good decisions, as the higher brain areas that deal with such matters do not develop when one is young, and are not activated even when they are somewhat developed. I went to one of the best high schools in the country, but was unable to take advantage of it; something I realized at the time with deep regret, though I did not know exactly why. I have read several psychological and neurobiological works that have explained in great detail what happens inside the human brain and mind when a child is abused.

The brain is a most incredible thing, with 100 billion cells, each cell capable of making connections with up to 10,000 other cells. How a child is treated determines what connections are made in his or her brain, and what structures in it are then activated as he reacts and relates to others. There are brain structures designed to help a person survive dangerous situations and environments, and these are the ones that get developed and connected in an abused child. Nature intended these structures to be engaged only intermittently, in the presence of an occurring threat, but for one who is constantly bombarded with abuse, these structures become overactive and do not turn off, creating a state of hypervigilance which results in a faster heart rate and higher blood pressure, eventually adversely affecting the kidneys, liver, digestive tract, and other organs and tissues of the body as well. Over time, it eventually leads to early sickness and disease for the individual. And those connections also determine what core beliefs the child holds about people and society and finally, how he behaves in, or reacts to, the world around him. It also determines what is valued in life. To his dying day, my father valued strength and brute force, the ability to outfight any other; to be able to inflict pain and strike terror in the hearts of others. For much of my life I was somewhat like him, though I graduated from badly wanting to be so very strong that no one could hurt me, to becoming so wealthy that I was untouchable. Fortunately, I did not achieve either of these things, for I have learned under Dr. Ramirez' tutelage that physical strength and great wealth are not what make a person strong. They also do not make a person a good one, or guarantee him happiness. And they certainly do not assure that he will be a benefit to society in any way.

There are many other circumstances that can cause a child to be sickly, so I don't want you to think that I'm saying that every sickly child is an abused one, for such is certainly not the case. But I know a man who is certain that his Type II diabetes is the result of the great anger he has stored up inside of himself, because he was badly abused as a child. I myself needed by-pass surgery at age 53 due to the very stressful life the abuse caused me to have, even though I was very physically active and exercised almost all of my life. And stents needed to be placed in my arteries three times after that. It is also next to impossible to live a happy, joyful life, living with such anxiety and tension; though there can be happy moments in it. One of my coping skills, when things got very bad for me, was to find something humorous in the situation and to actually laugh about it.

Within the brain there are other, communally oriented structures, that allow human beings to both work and to play together. These, higher in the brain structures, promote cooperative behaviors and intimacy within us, allowing us to establish peaceful and friendly relationships in our families and communities, and within the world at large. These structures also connect to the higher faculties of the cerebral cortex, the part of the brain that separates us from all other animals. The cerebral cortex allows humans to develop culture and society, to create and appreciate music, art, and drama. Here, humans developed, and continue to develop, language. Because of language, disciplines such as math, science, and philosophy were also able to be developed and elaborated upon. The cerebral cortex gives us the ability to think, to reason well, to imagine, to reach beyond ourselves, and to achieve great accomplishments. Sadly, these structures go largely undeveloped and remain dormant in a person who has been abused as a child, for his fear and anger absorb all of his time and energy, and activate only the brain structures beneath the cerebral cortex.

But there is good news: The brain, a most marvelous creation, perhaps the most complex structure in the universe, operating on both electrical and chemical energy, each cell a computer on its own, and as a whole, much more powerful and capable than any supercomputer, is "plastic." The connections that are made between the cells in it can be altered, again and again, as long as a person lives. Old connections can be diminished and extinguished, and new connections can be made. It happens slowly, at least at first, but it can and does happen. This is how therapy works, the only way it can work. It changes the connections in the brain.

My first and only female therapist helped me to understand some things. Foremost was that my number one goal in life was to have great friends, like I had when I was a little boy. In addition to this, she also helped me to see that I needed to become a much better man in order to achieve this goal. At first, I chose to emulate other men I knew while growing up, that I admired for the good they had done in our community, unlike my father; then I sought to become a therapist like her and Dr. Ramirez. When that didn't work out, I was left with just being myself. Finally, I am getting comfortable with being me, though it has taken till age 72 to achieve this.

Perhaps the cruelest effect of child abuse is that the child is unhappy with himself as he perceives his father is unhappy with him. In essence, the abused child cannot be a friend to himself. He cannot treat himself with care simply because he or she has never experienced care, and also does not consider himself or herself worthy of it. He takes unnecessary risks, abuses his body, either with over-exercising and consequently suffering painful injuries; or by abusing food and other substances, and suffering the harmful consequences they cause. He tries to live in the extreme to overcome what he considers to be his deficits. I tried this type of living. Ultimately it is self-defeating. And it is painful physically, as well as being mentally exhausting. Sometimes, it is also dangerous. I was literally competing with everyone I came into contact with, and competing always with myself the most. Always trying to go faster and faster, to accomplish more and more, I could never slow down or relax as my mind raced faster and faster. My muscles became so tense they always hurt.

Abuse can take many forms: verbal, called psychological abuse; physical abuse, including sexual abuse; and both physical and emotional neglect. All forms of abuse are harmful and in abundance, devastating; and their effects last a lifetime. I was in a restaurant one Saturday morning and seated a short distance away was a man and his young son. So engrossed with whatever he was looking at on his smartphone was he that his son was ignored the entire meal. I felt very sorry for the young boy. I wonder what he took away from that experience.

Our children are our most valuable possession and they deserve the very best of ourselves and all of our resources. It is from them that we, as parents, receive the greatest benefits in life. They are constant sources of joy and happiness. And they provide companionship and often support, as we age. I think that discovering who they are, rather than trying to mold them into what we think they should be, is the best way to parent. Find out what their talents and interests are and provide them with the resources with which they can develop them. They will be thankful you did and love you for it.

Another thing my female therapost was able to help me understand was that I had been an abused child, a severely abused one; something I had never considered myself as being, so caught up in fantasizing that I was a powerful, indominable force was I. And she helped me understand that it was adversely affecting my life. Furthermore, she taught me some skills to cope with less than optimum circumstances and situations and predicted that my life could become very good. Her prediction is finally coming true.

Some mental health experts are calling child abuse the #1 health crisis in America, due to the ailments and diseases caused by it to its victims; resulting in more frequent trips to the doctor and the hospital. The anger and rage stored inside a person who has been abused also sometimes leads to substance abuse and acts of violence on their part, resulting in jail time and/or prison sentences. Studies have shown the great difference in health at certain ages in life between people who have been abused versus those who have not been abused. The results are staggering and not pretty. They are also very costly, to the abused person, and to society as a whole. A certain psychiatrist, Bessel Van Der Kolk, M. D., has discovered that a much larger proportion of our nation's veterans who are suffering from mental illness experienced some form of abuse before they entered military service and mainly joined the military to escape it. I was one such person.

An immensely important thought to consider concerning child abuse is the great loss to society of the contributions that so many abused people would have been able to make to it, if they had been able to grow up normally as loved and valued children and then adults. We cannot begin to imagine what these people might have achieved in their lifetimes; the advances to society in so many ways that they might have made, rather than the drains upon it because of fits of rage that resulted in the police being called, and in jail and prison sentences. And also, the early ailments and diseases these people suffer that result in more, and higher, medical bills must be considered. These things are a constant drain on society's resources. Where might societies and civilization be now, in the absence of child abuse? Perhaps saddest of all, none of this is the abused person's fault. I labored for years under the assumption that I was first a bad child, and then a bad person, only to discover that it was never true; that I was a good son, very obedient 98% of the time, and am now a good person.

I have included some information about how the brain functions so that you may understand that all experiences create connections in our brains and once these connections are made, they establish patterns of thinking and behavior. For the same reason New Year's resolutions are so hard to keep, these established patterns are at first difficult to change. I kept this information to a minimum for fear of boring some readers, but I find the brain such a complex and fascinating structure; and as it is the source of everything about us, I have been intensely reading about it for three plus years now. For those who also find how our minds work interesting, I would encourage you to study about it. There is no end to the material that can be found on the internet, and so many good books on the market are available. And it can be studied on many different levels, accommodating whatever level of interest one has. I, myself, had to begin at a rather elementary level as the vocabulary and terminology were unfamiliar to me, but slowly I was able to gain knowledge so that now I am able to read on a more elevated level the writings of psychiatrists and neuroscientists.

Finally, I want to say that while my pronouns are predominantly masculine, because I was thinking about my own experiences as I wrote this, everything in this book applies to girls and women as well. Please don't think I don't know that girls and women are abused as much as boys and men, or even more so. I do. And my heart goes out to them for I have seen instances of how much they are made to suffer and some of the predicaments that are thrust upon them.

And now, some of the experiences I had with my father that had such a disastrous effect on me:

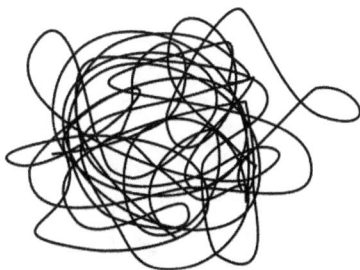

CHAPTER 1

The Thunderstorm and the Belt

When I was three or four, we lived in a tiny, one bedroom cottage. My brother and I slept in the bedroom and my parents slept on a hide-a-bed in the living room. One night, after my brother and I had gone to bed, a violent thunderstorm occurred. The lightening brilliantly lit up the room and the booming thunder badly frightened me. Very scared, I turned on our bedroom light. A few minutes later my father, having seen light coming from under the door, burst through it and demanded to know why the light was on. I told him, "I'm afraid of the thunder and lightning." "That's ridiculous," he said, "Turn out the light!" I did, but a few minutes later, my fears overwhelmed me again and caused me to turn the light back on a second time. When he burst through the door again, he took off his belt and whipped me twice with it. "Turn off the light and keep it off," he roared. This time I did. Those two whippings, the first I ever received, shocked me to my core. I was now more afraid of him than I was of God and Mother Nature. This taught me that men are to be feared more than God.

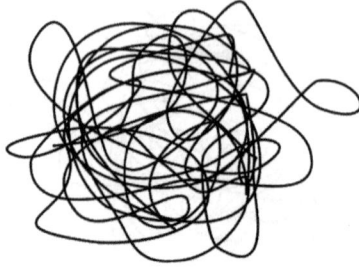

CHAPTER 2
Playing Horsey

Again, at age three or four, I used to stand on the chair beside our front door and jump up on my father's back when he came home from work. He would then ride me around on his shoulders. This got started when I first stood on the chair to greet him and he swung me around onto his shoulders. My father seemed to enjoy this as much as I did, until one evening he didn't. Grabbing me by my left arm, he swung me over his shoulder and flung me down on the floor, hard. I just lay there having landed flat on my back, unhurt but badly dazed and stunned. I could not comprehend what had happened and to this day have no idea what I was thinking or feeling. Whatever it was I knew enough not to ever jump on his back again, for I never did. This taught me that men are volatile, liable to change rapidly and unpredictably, most often for the worse.

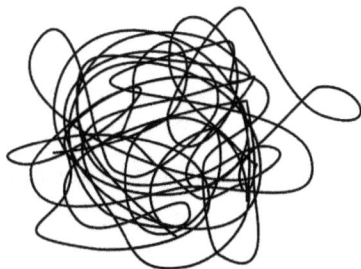

CHAPTER 3
PLAYING "HANDSIES"

My father insisted that my year and a half younger brother and I attend church services in the sanctuary from the
time I was four, even though they had classes for children in the
classrooms downstairs, which I begged to attend. "No," was the
answer. "I sat in church as a little boy and you are going to, also."
Our minister, who had a PhD in theology preached in lofty words.
Of course, my brother and I didn't understand most of them and
were soon bored. At the beginning of the sermons, my father,
who sat between us, would slouch down in the pew so that there
was space behind his back. Soon my brother and I were playing
handsies behind him. We became more and more aggressive until
our father noticed, and in severe annoyance fiercely whispered for
us to stop it and behave. This bad behavior resulted in a beating
for both of us with his belt, when we got home. After several such
Sunday church services and subsequent beatings, we were actually beaten before we went to church one time. When I became
16 and could drive, I told my parents that I wanted to attend the
9:30 a.m. service. We had always attended the 11:00 o'clock one
and my parents continued to do so. After attending the 9:30 service for a couple of weeks with my brother and noticing that our

parents never asked us about the service, we quit attending and just drove around for an hour. We were never caught. This and other experiences taught me that my father really didn't care what I did as long as it didn't cause him to suffer embarrassment and or cost him any money.

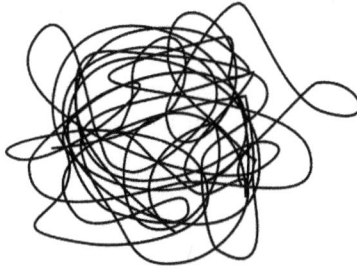

CHAPTER 4
The Nosebleed

My mother, who fed and clothed me, did little else for me. She never hugged or kissed me. She also never played with me or talked to me. I spent my days in our little house watching whatever she was doing. In the morning I watched her cook and can food. Later, I watched the Arthur Godfrey show with her. After lunch we watched Secret Storm, Guiding Light, Search for Tomorrow, and Queen for a Day. But between lunch and the soap operas there was about forty-five minutes. My mother would bring out my box of blocks for me to play with. She never helped me build anything and she never commented on anything I made. When the soaps were about to start, she always said to me, "Put your blocks back in the box." Being tired of erecting great buildings and bridges with which to impress her, I often asked her to help me. She never did. After the Soap Operas were over, she would sit at her piano and play. She was pretty good at what she played, Moonlight Serenade and other songs like it; but there was a bar or two in every piece that she always stumbled over. She would then play through the difficult bars until she got them right, but the next day would always stumble over them again. When I was in my 60s, I told her about it, and she laughed and said, "You really remember that?"

Anyway, I would always kneel just behind the piano bench and listen to her play as I enjoyed listening to the music. I rested my nose on the edge of the piano bench to listen. One day, she suddenly rocked back and the piano bench caught me squarely in the nose. Blood flowed everywhere. She had me lie on my back on the floor with my feet propped up, then she brought me ice wrapped in a dish towel that I held to my nose. That evening my father brought a man from work and his wife home for dinner. When they were all about to sit down, I told him I wasn't hungry and didn't feel good, and asked if I could go lie down. My mother had told him what had happened to me. "No," he said, "You're going to eat dinner with the rest of us." The prayer was said, and as I was chewing my first mouthful of food, blood gushed from my nose again, filling my plate. The process of lying on the floor holding a towel full of ice to my nose was repeated. After dinner, my father paraded us all out to the backyard where he started kicking the two footballs we had up in the air, directing me to catch them. Still dizzy from the lack of blood and weak from not eating, I only got close enough to the descending footballs so that a few bounced off me, but I caught none. Mercifully he soon kicked both footballs up into our trees, where they stayed, and I was spared further aggravation. I remember the man and his wife standing together, off to the side, whispering to one another as they looked on. This taught me that I was of no consequence and my needs were not important; that I was expected to be a performing seal.

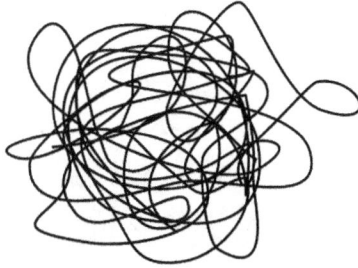

CHAPTER 5

Going to Marv Meek's Gas Station

On Saturday mornings, my father took me on his weekly jaunts to the gas station, owned by a high school friend, a few miles from our house. My parents had graduated from high school about 10 miles away from the gas station, and like many of their high school friends, had settled down close by. To me their friends were wonderful. We use to go to one of their homes every fourth of July for a picnic, where I made a pig of myself. They were always kind to me when I saw them in church and at the picnics. Anyway, I was the only child ever at the gas station and was totally ignored. I have no idea why my father took me. It was a long couple of hours, not having anything to do or anyone to talk to. Almost to his dying day my father bragged about punching a former Army serviceman there, who he said was always bragging about how tough he was. My father claimed he knocked him down the flight of stairs. And he always asked me, when he told the story which he was very fond of telling, if I remembered it. I didn't but said I did. This taught me that I was just a prop and should be a yes man.

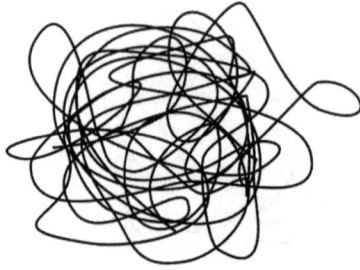

CHAPTER 6

Taking My Bike to Our New House

When I was six, the judge whose cottage we were renting, announced that he had built a house for us about a mile from where we lived. It was a nice house, two stories high with 3 bedrooms and one and a half baths. It also had a basement and a garage. When we moved, instead of making an extra trip to get the bike that was given to me by the judge's daughter (a girl's bike), my father held onto the left handle bar of the bike while I rode it as my mother drove the car. I was six at the time. To say that I was afraid of falling off of the bike at 20 miles per hour is an understatement. My father had me ride a girl's bike for two years in our new neighborhood after that. Luckily, nobody made fun of me, maybe because on our first evening there, when I was being taken around to be introduced to the kids in the neighborhood by the girl next door, a boy my age decided to hit me for some reason. I blocked his punch and knocked him flat on his back with a left hook to his face. The bike ride taught me that my life had little meaning or value, and that I was of no concern, certainly not if it meant making another trip. To put it mildly, I was expendable.

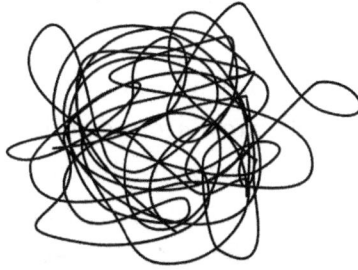

CHAPTER 7
Building the Wall

My father and my maternal grandfather put in our front yard at our new house with me picking up the smaller rocks and putting them in our wheelbarrow so they could be hauled to the back yard. They picked up the larger rocks. After they seeded the lawn, my father's vacation time was over and back to work he went. Summer had come and I was out of school. He told me to build a retaining wall along our driveway behind the house next to the garage, to keep the hillside dirt from falling into the driveway. It only had to be a ten-foot-long wall about four-feet high. But the wall was to be built with the irregular rocks that had been pulled out of where the foundation of the house was poured by the construction crew, and the rocks that had been pulled out of the yard by my father, grandfather and me. They had all been piled up in the lower, far corner of our back yard, about one-hundred feet from where the wall was to be built. The backyard had been only roughly graded, and was uneven dirt and mud. The path from where the rocks lay to where the wall was to be built was slightly uphill. *And*, I was only six years old.

The first morning of my attempt, I took the wheelbarrow out of the garage down to where the stones were. I knew this was going to be hard work but I had a positive outlook on it. "I will build the wall!" Turning the wheelbarrow around so it headed in the direction of the driveway when I got to the rocks, I loaded the four largest rocks I could pick up into the wheelbarrow. Larger rocks meant fewer rocks to build the wall, and fewer rocks meant fewer trips. Or so I thought. Trying to pick up on the handle bars, I couldn't get the wheelbarrow skids off of the ground. The rocks were simply too heavy. I took out a rock and heaved mightily upward again. The skids came slightly off the ground, but with two rocks on one side and only one rock on the other, the wheelbarrow was unbalanced, and tipped over to the heavier side, spilling out all three rocks. I was getting a harsh lesson in physics. This time I put only two rocks in the wheelbarrow. Unfortunately, I put them in the middle of it, one behind the other. It was still heavy, but I could move forward, until the uneven muddy ground caused the wheelbarrow to tip sideways. This caused the rocks to slide to one side. The uneven weight was too much for my arms and over went the wheelbarrow on its side, the rocks again spilling out on the ground. Now tiring and becoming somewhat dismayed, I righted the wheelbarrow and put the two rocks, this time side by side, into it. It was still a struggle to get the skids off of the ground, but I managed and went forward, for about five feet. A hard clump of dirt stopped the wheel abruptly, the handlebars twisted in my hands again, and over went the wheelbarrow, spilling the rocks out a third time. More dismayed and growing weak, I righted the wheelbarrow yet again and put the rocks back in, struggling. I now remembered that either my father or grandfather had said that putting the weight over the wheel made it easier to pick up on the handlebars, so I put the two rocks side by side in he very front of the wheelbarrow and found that it was true. I moved forward easily, much heartened, until the wheel hit another clump of dirt and the handlebars lifted straight up out of my hands as the wheelbarrow tipped over forward. Gloom descended upon me like a fog and my mind was beginning to fill with despair. I sat in the dirt awhile to rest. "I'm not seeing much work being done out there," the voice of a little boy's biggest fan came from the kitchen window. "Your father is not going to be very happy." Gripped by fear, I righted the wheelbarrow, put the two rocks side by side in the middle of it, and moved forward. But the same thing kept happening over and over, as the uneven ground, the small rocks or clumps of hard dirt, caused me to lose control of the handle-bars and over the wheelbarrow would go. I did finally get those two rocks to the driveway and was going back for more when my mother called from the window, saying that it was time for lunch.

Sitting in the kitchen, glumly eating my peanut butter and jelly sandwich, I just blankly stared at the table. My mother told me she had called my father and that he was very unhappy with my lack of progress. Saying nothing, I slowly went back outside to the rockpile. Throughout much of the afternoon I continued to work, with the same results. No matter how many rocks I put in the wheelbarrow, or how I arranged them, they always slid around when the wheel hit something and over went the wheelbarrow. I had six rocks at the wall site but could not stack them, so irregular were they. When my father came home, he ripped into me, so I told him about the uneven ground and how it always caused the wheelbarrow to tip over. "Well," he said, "I'll put some boards down and you can roll the wheelbarrow on them." Unfortunately, the boards he chose were 2x4s, so narrow it was impossible for me to keep the wheel on them. As he just dropped them on the ground and did not press them into it, they canted to one side or the other according to the dirt underneath them, as the wheel of the wheelbarrow rolled over them. This caused the wheel to come off the board and the wheelbarrow to tip over. Since the boards were worse than just the dirt itself, I finally pushed them out of the way. The rest of the day I struggled on, with only a few rocks to show for my effort. That night, my father came home, yelled at me, took off his belt and whipped me. I cried myself up to my room. Day three brought a severe admonition to finally do some work, or else. Very anxious now, I headed to the garage and took out the wheelbarrow. A brilliant idea came to mind. "Why not build the wall out of the small rocks?" Really heartened now, I partially filled the wheelbarrow with some of the smallest rocks and wheeled them up to the wall site. It was easy. But when I tried to stack them on top of one another, they being as irregular as the larger rocks and with very little surface area, I could only add a second rock on top of the first in a very wobbly manner. Another lesson in physics was learned: Bigger rocks must be on the bottom. Getting a third rock to stay on top of the first two little rocks was simply out of the question. I'm certainly no genius, but it did not take a genius to see that I could not build a wall beginning with the small rocks.

Back to trying to get the larger rocks into the wheelbarrow and up to the driveway, I made very little progress that day. My father came home. Off came his belt and I was whipped again. I could not find the words to explain to him what was happening with the 2x4s he had laid down. The next morning, he again told me he expected to see real progress that day. With no enthusiasm for the job left inside me, I started the fourth day. It was more of the same, only worse. My hands were raw from struggling with the rough rocks, for my father had not provided me with gloves; and my little muscles were very tired and aching. As the wheelbarrow kept tipping over time after time, a deep numbness and dark gloom settled in on me, so thick it could have been cut with a knife. I finally sat down on the ground, put my left elbow on my knee, then my head in my hand and just sat there. Again, my mother's voice called from the kitchen window, "I don't see much work being done. Just wait till your father gets home. Are you going to get it!" "So," I thought glumly, still just sitting there, "this is to be my life. There's no way out!" A feeling of hopeless wretchedness, deep despair, and utter dejection came over me, so dark and heavy that I could not move for a long while. Again, I was beaten that night and went to my room whimpering. The fifth day I made no attempt to build the wall, staying in my room the entire day. My father finally gave up on me and built the damn wall himself.

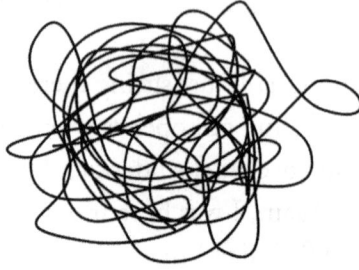

CHAPTER 8

Climbing Telephone Poles

The above, Building the Wall, experience, taught me that I was not good enough in the eyes of my father and therefore could not meet his expectations and earn his acceptance and love. It also taught me a larger lesson; that acceptance and love are very conditional. This led to me to do things that I could do, but were a reaction to my father's rejection of me. And some of the things I chose to do to bolster my opinion of myself were unnecessary, often risky and very painful, and therefore should not have been done. Right after my failure to build the wall, I watched a Bell Telephone man climb the telephone pole on our property line to repair something. He had a large spur on the inside of each of his boots that dug into the pole, and a heavy belt around his waist that also encircled the pole so that he did not have to hug it, in order to hang on; briefly stated, he had the tools for the job.

The next day, I went out to the same pole and shinnied up it. Having no spurs or belt, I had to hug the pole with my arms and legs and shinny up it. The pole was very rough and I got large splinters in my arms and legs, and abrasions on them and my stomach as well. I had to pull the splinters out and it took some weeks for the pain from them and the abrasions to subside. It was only due to the fact that my grandfather had taught me about electricity that I did not climb as high as the Bell man did and electrocute myself. You would think that one such painful experience would have been enough, but as soon as the pain subsided, I was out climbing that damn pole again, reinjuring myself. Was I punishing myself? Or proving to myself that I could do hard and painful work? I truly do not know, but I spent the rest of the summer doing it.

This story is an example of what was said earlier; that abuse victims do not know how to take care of themselves since their abusers did not take care of them, and they will take unnecessary risks, even harming themselves, to prove their self-worth. It is a most unfortunate thing.

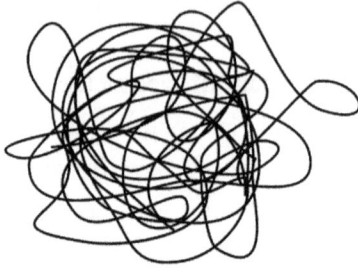

CHAPTER 9
Cutting the Grass

The grass had grown in our front yard by my seventh summer and needed to be cut. Our lot was half an acre, so there was not quite a quarter of an acre to be cut as our back yard was the larger of the two. My father brought my grandfather's motorless reel push mower home on a Sunday after we visited him, and told me to cut the grass with it. The following Monday morning I went out and tried to mow the grass. I simply could NOT push the lawn mower. It was old, in bad need of sharpening and of being cleaned and oiled. I took about five running starts at it but it would only travel eight or ten feet until it stopped. After missing the handlebars with my hands a few times and catching them in my stomach, which hurt, I finally gave up. Home came my father that night, off came his belt, 6 more whacks were added to my butt. After dinner he went out to cut the grass, and finally gave up. The next weekend he bought an old, used reel mower with a motor, and a different kind of problem presented itself. My father showed me how to start the mower - pull out the choke, wrap the cord around the flywheel, pull the cord, and it would start, or so he said. After half an hour of fiddling with the carburetor screws, he finally got it to start and let me cut the grass with it for a minute or two. Then because it was getting dark, he shut it off and said, "When I come home from work tomorrow, I expect the grass to be cut."

The next morning, I went out full of hope, pulled the choke out, wrapped the starter cord around the pulley and yanked. Nothing happened. I wrapped the cord around the pulley and pulled harder. Again and again, I tried, but it simply would not start. Home came my father, off came his belt, red and sore became my butt. Up to my room I went, to soothe my aching spirit. We went out after dinner and he tried to start the lawn mower. Nothing. After an hour of adjusting the 2 carburetor screws, it finally started when it had become quite dark. He shut it off. "There," he said, "it will start for you in the morning." Only it didn't. I yanked and yanked on the starter cord till there was no yank left in me. Into the house I came. "Why aren't you cutting the grass?" my mother asked. "I can't get the mower started," I said. She looked at me very disapprovingly and said, "Come on," and outside we went to the lawn mower. On her third pull of the cord, the lawn mower started. I was humiliated. "Cut the grass," she said; and I did. The next week, when it was again time to cut the grass, the same thing happened. Only this time she couldn't start the mower either. And so it went, week after week for two summers. I would try to start the mower and couldn't; my father would tinker with the carburetor settings all evening before it started, and the next day it wouldn't start; usually on Saturday morning he would get it started and I would then cut the grass. After two years he finally got tired of this ridiculous routine and bought a new rotary lawnmower with a powerful engine and I cut the grass from then on with it and its replacements, until I left for the Air Force at age nineteen.

But all was not peaceful yet. We had a place in our yard where the grass grew several times higher than in the rest of it, because it was over the leech bed that was a marsh full of stagnant sewage water. It took me a long time to cut all of the grass within it. Consequently, my shoes and socks would be soaked and full of grass, and stinking. After cutting the grass, I would put the lawn mower away and sit on our side steps to remove my shoes and socks before entering the house. No matter where I was in this process, my father would always come up to me and growl, "Make sure you take your shoes and socks off before you go inside!"

As a child, I failed to understand that my father's cruelness was fully inside of him and that I was in no way responsible for it. As a result, both the unfairness of it and its cruelty became a part of me. I recognized even then that him telling me to take off my shoes and socks before entering the house, even as I was doing it, was absurd, but my young mind was unable to ward off the effects of it. This was on account of not having "firm walls" or "good boundaries." This is something I talk about in my second book, *Lessons My Mother Taught Me,* which is also about child abuse.

A final note about the yard. When we moved to Crestview Drive, I made friends with both children my age and the older boys I played sports with, similar to the two sets of friends I had at our former house. One boy in particular, in between both age groups, became good friends with me. His father owned a rototiller and my friend said he could bring it up to our house so that my father could till the backyard (the larger part of our yard) so that grass could be planted. My father said okay and that's how our backyard got finished. My father never thanked me for that, even though he did thank my friend.

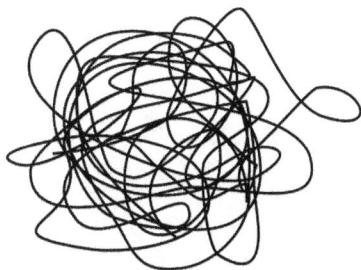

CHAPTER 10
Boxing Lessons

From who knows where, my father got leather, 8-ounce, real pro-fessional boxing gloves made by Everlast. On Saturday mornings, when I was eight years old, before cutting the grass, he would take me down to the basement to give me boxing lessons. He taught me to keep my guard up with my right hand (I'm left-handed) and punch with my left. After a few minutes of him gently sparring with me he would turn his left side to me and say, "Go ahead, punch me in the arm as hard as you can," so I did. Each time I hit him he would say, "That doesn't hurt," so I would try to hit him even harder. After three or four punches he would suddenly spin and punch me full in the face as hard as he could, lifting me up off my feet and sending me sailing through the air across our basement. Somehow, I never got hurt when I landed on the concrete floor. Sadly, after a few episodes of this, I was doing the same thing out in the back yard with my younger brother. After the first time, he pleaded with me not to make him box me again. After the second time I never did it to him again, but it was too late – the damage was done and he has never forgotten it nor I suspect, forgiven me for it, even though I have apologized and explained to him that it was exactly the same thing our father was doing to me. And we are now in our 70s.

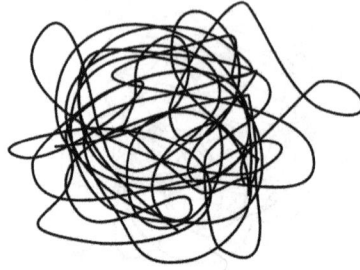

CHAPTER 11
Going Crazy

One time my father had his belt off and was about to whip me. It was so undeserved that I turned my head around to face him and gave him the most impudent look I could manage. He immediately went crazy. Intensely angry and out of control of himself, he started whipping me as fast as he could as we danced around in circles. Out of habit, I started crying even while realizing this out-of-control whipping wasn't hurting me very much. From this, I learned that his whippings were a control and power trip for him, and that I was his whipping boy. Though tempted to look back at him impudently the next time he was about to whip me, I didn't. Unfortunate? Who can say. He might have killed me.

It was also the case that sometimes he knew he had gone too far, and then he would want to play a game of gin or checkers, thinking this would make it up to me. However, it only made me angrier and I would play so badly that it was obvious what I was doing, and then he would appear to have his feelings hurt. He never figured out that if he just broke the cycle of abuse, there would be no need for this.

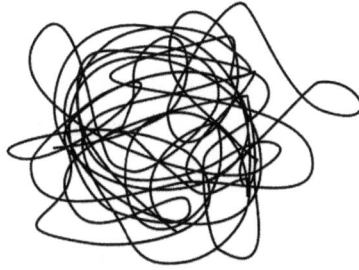

CHAPTER 12

Asking for Second Helpings

D inner was served in our dining room around a large round table. I sat to my father's right. While most of the food was in serving dishes from which we helped ourselves, the meat was always on a platter in front of my father. He cut slices for each of us and placed them on our plates with the fork and carving knife he used to cut the meat. His portions to me were the same size as they were to my mother and my brother, both of whom were not nearly as active as me. When I asked for a second helping of meat, I usually got it, but every so often I got back-handed, hard, across the face; and asking for a third helping was always a 50-50 proposition. Yet even though I knew this to be so, it never stopped me from asking if I was still hungry. One time he back-handed me so hard that I went over backwards in my chair.

Years of being smacked in the face resulted in my face being numb all the time and in me losing control of my facial muscles. It has caused me to smile and laugh at inappropriate times if I found an occurrence to be even sightly humorous, even though I knew it was

21

not a situation to be smiled or laughed at. This has often been very embarrassing for me, for people look at me strangely and I know they think less of me.

My younger brother, who never asked for seconds, ran afoul of my father in a different way. Whenever my father spilled something, he would always say, "O darn, look what I've done" and then clean it up. One time my brother, as a 10-year-old and sitting to my father's left, knocked over his milk during dinner. My father slapped him so hard that he and his chair fell over backwards. My father was ambidextrous when it came to smacking us. Then he ordered my brother to clean it up and finish his dinner in the kitchen. After dinner he told my brother he had to eat in the kitchen for a week. When the week was up, my father ordered him back to the dining room table. "Can't I eat in the kitchen?" my brother asked in fear. "No," my father roared, "you eat in here now." His first dinner back in the dining room, my poor brother ate his dinner but did not touch his glass of milk. Finally, my father noticed this and said, "drink your milk," in a commanding voice. My brother slowly reached for his glass of milk, his hand shaking so badly that I didn't see how he could do anything but knock it over. I feared for him. Miraculously he managed to drink it without spilling it.

I figured out during my years of therapy to get over what the abuse had done to me, that as a child, I had been able to feel sorrier for my brother and our younger foster sister, when they were being abused, than I had been for myself. I very much recognized how horrible were the things our parents did to them, but for myself I felt nothing. Indeed, it was almost two years into therapy before I began to understand that I had been a severely abused child, a mere punching bag and whipping boy, and then little by little I began to comprehend how that had limited me in my life, allowing others to take advantage of me and abuse me, for I thought I was of no value and agreed to almost anything; and then the rage inside of me started to come out. It was so intense that it frightened me badly, for several years, for I knew the damage that my rage could do to others.

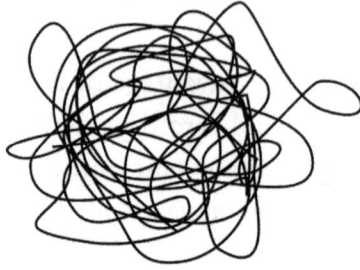

CHAPTER 13

"You Are Wasting My Electricity!"

THE REFRIGERATOR

At noon one day, I was hungry and headed for the kitchen. Once there, I opened the refrigerator door and looked inside for something to eat. Almost immediately my father came up from behind me, slammed the door shut hard, and yelled, "You're wasting my electricity! Know what you want and know where it is in the refrigerator before you open that door!" This taught me that I needed to have supernatural powers to see inside of things like refrigerators if I was going to get along in his world.

GOING IN & OUT

Any time I went outside, or came indoors, I didn't move fast enough according to him, which is hard to believe since I was the fastest moving person in our family, if not the entire neighborhood. Each time I opened the door he would yell, "Hurry up, you're wasting my electricity. Close that door!" The funny thing is, in the evening during winter when the heat was on, he would open up both doors and windows, "to blow the stink out," as he expressed it, to get fresh air into the house every night. He left them open until it was very cold inside, which burned more electricity to heat the house up again than was used by me entering and leaving the house for the entire year. I had the good sense not to point this out to him.

"YOU'RE WEARING OUT MY CARPET!"

Anytime I went up or down the stairs, he would scream, "You're wearing out my carpet! Don't put your feet down in the center of the stair, walk on the sides of the stair." I retaliated by sliding down the middle of the stairs on my butt, when he wasn't around. I was after all, just a kid!

"YOU'RE WEARING OUT MY PUMP!"

Our house had a well with a submersible pump. Anytime I ran water, it was always too much. I used too much water to do the dishes, too much water to wash my face and hands, and way too much water to take a bath. So over and over again he would scream, "Turn that water off, you're wearing out my pump!" His idea of me taking a bath was to fill the tub with water so that there was a half inch in it where I sat down, which when I did this, I could feel the cold of the tub on my butt. I rebelled. When taking a bath, especially in the winter after delivering newspapers in temperatures below 10 degrees, I would fill the tub up full enough so that I could immerse my entire body under the water to thaw out, always when he couldn't hear me do it. I felt I deserved to do so. After all, my parents took from me every penny I earned delivering newspapers, while at the same time my father bragged to me that from the age of 13, he had bought all his clothes. I'm guessing he was able to do this because his parents weren't taking all of the money he earned.

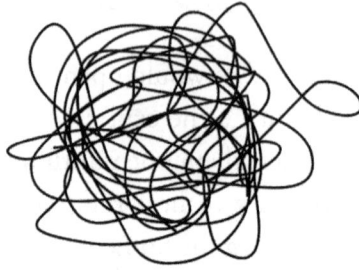

CHAPTER 14

"It Looks Like a Bird Cage Full of Canaries!"

I needed a new sports jacket to go to church in, as the sleeve ends of my current one were approaching my elbows. My mother said to me, "You are going shopping with us to buy you a new sports jacket." "Can't you just go and buy me one," I said, "you know my size." "Why don't you want to go?" she asked. "You never buy what I want," I said. "I promise, you can pick out what you want," was her reply. Very skeptical, I reluctantly rode down to Gimbels with my parents. Entering the boys' department, there was a wonderful brightly colored sports jacket. It had small, blue frames around yellow interiors. The yellow interiors had detail to them and were not just merely yellow. It was colorful and beautiful and I loved it immediately. "I want that one," I said. "Oh, we can't buy you that one," my mother said, "it looks ridiculous." I wondered then what my peers would think of it. Would they be envious or snickering behind my back? But I simply did not care. My parents were still making me wear white socks long after they went out of style and they bought me nothing trendy. "I don't care," I said, "you told me I could have the one I wanted and I want that one." And so it went, until the store was about to close, an hour and a half later.

At first the salesman was enthusiastic at making a sale, and even after the argument between my parents and I erupted, he tried to hurry the sales process along. Then, he would go away for a while and later come back, still hoping for the sale. As our argument continued unabated, he came back less and less often, but did give me sympathetic looks each time he came. In the end, I wound up with the dullest, drabbest jacket in the store. The lesson: People will lie to you anytime they want to get you to do what they want.

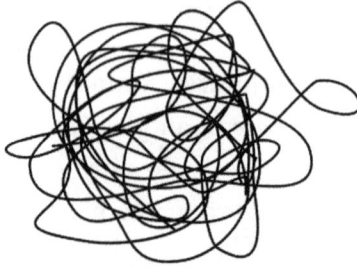

CHAPTER 15

"We're Using Your Money to Get There, So You've Got to Go Too"

My parents took every cent I made delivering papers and most of the money I made working at Islay's and Acme Supermarket. They did allow me enough money to buy gas so that I could get to and from work. Their rationale: "We're saving that money so you can go to college." It was the spring of 1966. I was sixteen. I had played Little League baseball since the age of nine, and two years before had won the first and third games of a three-game championship as the pitcher of my team. Don't get me wrong. I didn't win those games by myself. My teammates were excellent in the field and at bat, but I pitched good games – some one- and two-hitters. I had excellent control but just over average speed, so I knew baseball was not my future. The year before, in 1965, I played on a good team in Pony League that placed second. I liked my fellow players, the manager, and was ready for the season to start. It was then that my parents announced, "We're going to California this year." Four of my dad's brothers, his sister, and his mother lived in either Manhattan Beach or Redondo Beach. While I would have liked going, I preferred staying home to play baseball. I was sixteen, and had a job at a supermarket which I liked as well. "No," my mother said, "you have to come with us; after all, we're using your money to go." I don't know how long it was before I figured out that this was the money that they were taking from me, insisting that they were saving it so that I could go to college. My enthusiasm for life diminished at this point so that when I went to see my manager to tell him I couldn't play that year because I would be spending August in California, even though he told me I could still play and go on vacation, I declined. And of course, they won the championship. I never again played organized baseball. To top it off, my parents left me at an uncle's house and were out eating and drinking in restaurants and going to interesting places the whole time we were there, on my money. Lesson learned: People will rob you and have a good time with your money. I let some managers do that to me too, later in life.

This happened in 1966, the year of the airlines strike, when no planes were flying east of Chicago, and only Continental Airlines west of there. We got up very early in the morning to take a train to the Windy City from Pittsburgh, and suffered for eleven hours in an ancient, unheated coach that had been put into service to accommodate the additional passengers, on account of the strike. When we finally reached Chicago, my father immediately called O'Hare Airport from the train station to see when flights were taking off for Los Angeles. As he was calling, I said to my mother, "It makes no difference when planes are taking off if we're not at the airport. Let's get there first." Amazingly and maybe for the first time in my life, my mother agreed with me, saying, "The kid's right Rich, let's go to the airport now." I was now elevated from the "Son of Satan" to "the Kid", a great leap upward; but it was not to last very long.

We had driven to LA seven years earlier, when I was nine, and it had been a mixed bag though it held the biggest WOW moment of my life, seeing the Pacific Ocean while standing on the bank high above it, at Redondo Beach. The enormity of it simply overwhelmed me.

But back then, some of my cousins, my brother, and I played a game of tag in our grandmother's yard one evening after dinner. At one point, a cousin ran through a patch of ground ivy to avoid being tagged by me and badly tore it up. Our aunt, who lived with our grandmother, was furious. My father grabbed me, took me in the house and whipped me. Half an hour later, my brother climbed up a long slab of marble leaning on a thirty-degree angle against a railing, the result being it snapped in half. Again, my father's sister was furious, since she had a purpose for it. Though not even in the vicinity when it happened, I caught hell from my father again. His rational for both incidents: Since I was the oldest of all the kids, I should have prevented these things from happening. In his world I had to be able to control all events. But I wasn't God; not even close. I was just a kid!

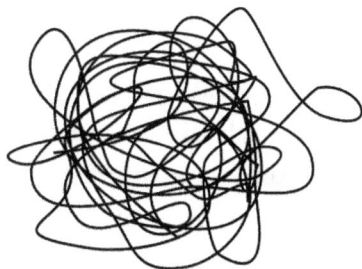

CHAPTER 16

"Can't You See He Wants to Go in His House!"

One Saturday afternoon, my father and I were at our church for some reason. This was a few years after my father had quit his job as the church's janitor. As we were leaving for home, a fellow member of our church was ready to go home also. Though he lived a short distance from the church by foot which is how he got there, my father offered him a ride and he accepted. The way to his house was much farther by car and along the way he was talking to my father, who said very little. As we neared his house, the man said something that caught my attention and interested me very much. I asked him a question about it, and turning in his seat to talk to me, he began explaining that which I had asked about. We were having a good conversation when my father pulled up and stopped in front of the man's home. After five seconds, my father cried out, "David, can't you see the man wants to go in his house!" The man turned in his seat and looked at the side of my father's face as my father stared straight out the windshield. He looked at him for a full five seconds, neither man saying anything. Then he finally said, "Thanks for the ride," and got out. As I write this the thought came to me that I could have looked up the man's phone number in our church directory when we got home and called him to see if he would continue our conversation. I never thought to do that back then. How awesome it would have been if he had been willing to talk to me!

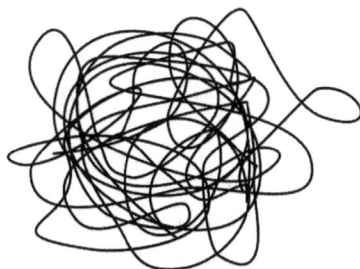

CHAPTER 17

"Rich, Get My ladder!"

About every three years our wooden gutters needed tarred on the inside and painted on the outside. The trim underneath the gutters, as well as the trim on the gable ends of the house needed painted as well. Parts of them often needed to be scraped and while doing so, I also scraped my knuckles. From the age of ten, this became my job, under the direction of my father, who stood at the base of the ladder. Ours was a two-story house, 3 stories over the driveway, the twenty-five-foot drop to the concrete always making me a little uncomfortable when I was on the ladder above it. My father and I would get our neighbor's extension ladder and raise it up just higher than the gutter. Then my father would open the can of tar and hand it and a paint brush to me, and up the ladder I'd go. To do the job properly, I had to angle the brush away from the roof to tar the gutters all the way up to the shingles that hung slightly over their top edges, and then I had to angle the brush the other way to tar the front portion of the gutter, which meant that the backs of my fingers were rubbing up against the edge of the shingles. This hurt quite a bit and after a while, certain portions of my fingers were raw and bleeding, for my father never provided me with gloves. I never complained, however. The painting was not quite as painful, but took longer. I was never thanked or taken to get ice cream or anything like that. And I never received an allowance for all the work I did.

One year, I ran out of paint about four feet short of the end of the gutter just outside my brother's and my bedroom window. We had taken our neighbor's ladder back to him by the time my father bought more paint. My father said to me, "Just crawl out the bedroom window with the brush in your teeth, stand on the window sill while holding on to the gutter and as I lift your legs in the air you reach out toward the end of the gutter and hold on." And that is what I did. There I was, outside my bedroom window in a horizontal position with my father holding my legs up with his right hand and reaching the paint can out the window with his left, while I hung on to the gutter with my left hand and painted with my right one. I definitely did not feel safe. To make matters worse, we had bushes with very strong stalks reaching up, ready to impale me if I fell the two stories down to them. Our neighbor, who was mowing his front lawn at the time, was apoplectic with anger and kept screaming at my father, "Rich, get my ladder!" My father didn't, and that is how the last four feet of our gutter got painted. Once again it taught me that my life was of little value, that I was expendable, and that I had to do every dangerous and insane thing that was asked of me.

A year or two later, our neighbor was up on his ladder painting the front of his house when his feet tired out and he slid down the ladder, receiving a tremendous jolt when he hit the ground. Though mainly unhurt except for sprained ankles, he was afraid to go back up the ladder and asked me to finish the painting, which I did. Sometime after that my mother told me that my father had complained to her saying, "Why is David always helping the neighbors and won't help me?" It was such a bogus statement that I wondered where in the world his mind was at when he made it.

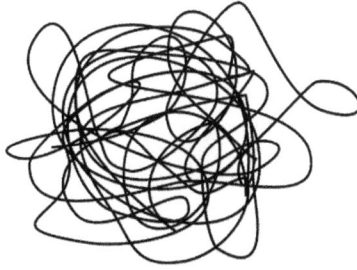

CHAPTER 18

"Don't Do as I Do; Do as I Say!"

In our upstairs bathroom, where we all washed up and brushed our teeth to get ready for the day, we had a plastic drinking cup with which to wash our mouths out with water after brushing our teeth. As we had very "hard" well water full of minerals, the cup was encrusted with mineral deposits and looked and smelled disgusting. My father never closed the bathroom door fully, even when he was going to the toilet (a habit I found strange and never copied), and so I saw him several times just duck his face under the faucet and take a mouthful of water directly from it. So, I started doing it. One day he barged into the bathroom, though I had closed the door, and saw me getting a mouthful of water directly from the faucet. "Use the cup," he bellowed. "That's what it's there for." Well, I didn't and sometime later he caught me again. This time he punched me in what I thought was my left arm so hard that I flew up against the far bath tub wall. Not thinking much about it (I guess I had accepted my role as a punching bag and just went numb), I went to school. Going to gym class, I took off my shirt to get into my gym clothes. "Where did you get that?" my gym teacher asked, in more of a demanding tone than an inquisitive one, pointing to my left side. I looked down and saw a huge, deep, dark, black and blue bruise the size of a volley ball. I stared blankly at it, not having the slightest idea how it got there. After gym class, I went to three more classes, straining my memory, until I finally figured it out. My mind had blocked the memory of the morning's incident, to protect me.

This is how an abused person is able to go on with his or her life, despite the abuse. Their mind mercifully blocks the abusive incidents from conscious memory. But these incidents are stored up in one's unconscious memory, along with the physical pain caused by them, as well as the fear of the abuser, which is sadly expanded in one's mind to include all people in general. And along with the pain, the fierce rage at being treated so badly is stored in the unconscious mind as well. It takes a lot of energy for the brain to keep these experiences from reaching conscious memory. And blocking destructive experiences leaves little or no energy for constructive thinking, which occurs in the uppermost portion of the brain, called the cerebral cortex, and most especially in the prefrontal lobes, right behind the eyes. Constructive thinking includes the ability to concentrate, study, plan, and conceptualize; in other words, to do abstract thinking. The abused person also has no mental energy left for creativity. So addled is a child's mind by abuse, he cannot concentrate or think clearly, to the point of not being able to learn from normal everyday experiences. I was unable to learn the usual lessons of life like most people. Therefore, I could not grow as a person, and so, seemed dull and stupid to most others. It is a most frustrating experience to know that you are not stupid, but are unable to act anyway but. I graduated in the bottom third of my high school class and only by intense effort was I able to make the Dean's List every semester, when I returned to college after serving in the Air Force.

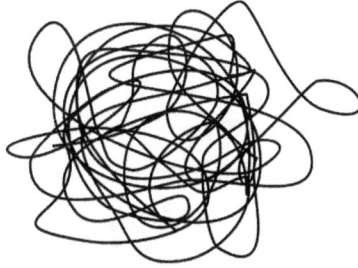

CHAPTER 19

"Move Your Hands!"

I never counted how many times my father slapped me in my face but it was easily more than one hundred over ten years' time. Ironically, I never knew it was coming, which tells me that I did not think I deserved it. He hit hard, but never satisfied to slap me just once, he would always raise his hand to strike me again. I always threw my hands up in front of my face to protect it. "Move your hands," he would roar at me." "What do you think I am, crazy?" I would shout back. Then he would grab at my hands, trying to pull them away from my face. As I moved my hands trying to prevent him from grabbing even one, he would try to get a good slap in, but self-preservation is strong in me and I was lightning fast, so that he almost never accomplished it. Even if he did manage to grab one of my hands, God gave me two of them, same as him, and I could always ward off a slap with just one hand. Some years ago, I wondered what was going through his mind, what was motivating him to always try to hurt me.

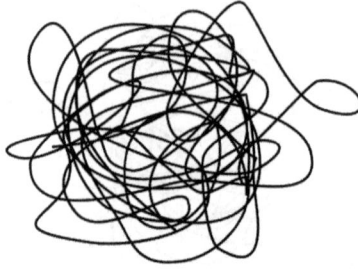

CHAPTER 20
"You're in the Way!"

Often my parents made me go food shopping with them and many times my father and I would be standing in an aisle across from one another while my mother was filling the cart with what she wanted. Sometimes we would be talking to each other and at other times we would just be standing there. If someone came in my direction from my blind side my father would roughly grab me by the arm and yank me toward himself, saying, "Can't you see, you're in the way!" This also often happened in front of our church entrance which had a large paved area where we stood, until my father felt it was time to go inside for the service. From these experiences, I learned that I was not entitled to one square foot on the earth, upon which to stand. Years later I wondered why the son of a bitch didn't just step over to my side of the aisle or pavement to let the other customers or worshipers pass by, since he could see them coming and I couldn't.

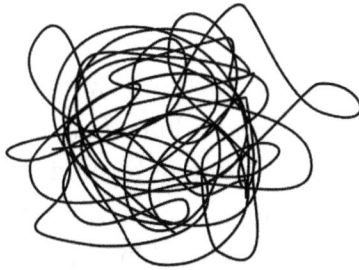

CHAPTER 21

"Do You See the Fear in His Eyes?"

As I've said before, my mother never hugged or kissed me or gave me credit for anything, even after once saving her from injury as a small child. One day she was trying to paddle me when I was about 12, with the inch thick, two-foot wooden paddle she had. It simply wasn't hurting me, and so she said to my father who was standing there watching us, "Why can't I hurt him?" My father took off his belt and said, "Here, try this," and so she did. For whatever reason I began jumping up, bending my legs at the knees and spinning in circles as my mother, who had hold of my right arm with her right hand, was trying to whip me. It was comical. My father and I were both laughing and my mother was wearing herself out. When she finally quit trying to hurt me, my father said to her, "Give me the belt." He grabbed me by my left arm with his left hand, pulled back the belt in his right hand, and gleefully said to her, like he had just conquered Mount Everest, "Do you see the fear in his eyes?" Perhaps this taught me that I was supposed to let others hurt me although I never enjoyed being hurt and as far as I know, avoided being hurt as much as possible.

My father was physically cruel in his whippings. He would whip me across my legs instead of on my butt. This really hurt, caused welts, and often broke the skin, resulting in blood dripping down the backs of my legs. When I complained to him one time, his response was, "Good, I want it to hurt." Another thing he said was most diabolical and could have been emotionally devastating to me, had I accepted it as being true. "You can only go so long without needing to be beaten," Yeah, like I think to myself, "Hey, I really need a good whipping today. Let's do something to really piss the old man off." I knew as soon as the words came out of his mouth that it was not true; that he needed to get his fear and anger out, so he beat on a smaller, weaker person (me) in order to feel like a man in control again. One thing I've learned in life: real men, strong men, will not hurt you if you don't screw with them. They know they are strong and tough and do not need to prove it to themselves or anyone else, so I always feel safe around strong men. By strong, I mean mentally, emotionally strong, not just physically strong.

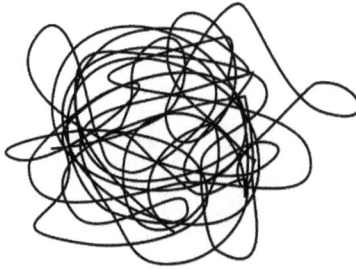

CHAPTER 22

What's the Matter, Do You Have a Guilty Conscience?"

Whenever my father was near me and made a sudden move, I would instinctively throw my hands up in front of my face, in a defensive posture as an act of self-defense. If my father did not intend to hit me, he would always say, "What's the matter, do you have a guilty conscience?" as though I thought I was guilty of something and deserved to be hit. Like I said, diabolical.

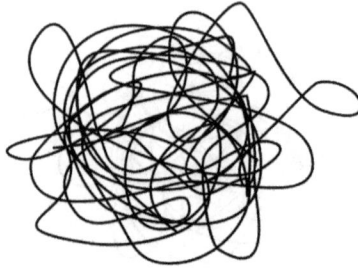

CHAPTER 23

Utensils, Flying Through the Air

One time we had company for dinner and our round table had been lengthened by three, foot-wide boards in the middle of its separated halves, to accommodate all of the guests. I believe they were people from one of the church groups, but only know for certain that they were not relatives. As always, I sat to my father's immediate right. During the meal, my father made a sudden movement with his right arm and I threw my hands up in front of my face to protect myself, my fork and knife leaving my hands, heading for the ceiling in a graceful arc that had them land in the middle of the table, clanking on the several serving dishes. All conversation stopped. In a very low voice, my father said to me, "What's the matter, did you think I was going to hit you?" Not certain what answer would ensure my continued survival, I said nothing. But conversation did not resume, so that my father asked more loudly, in a voice I'm sure all could hear, "Did you think I was going to hit you?" "Yeah," I said very softly, wondering what reaction from him this admission would bring. He said nothing more and our guests picked up my fork and knife and passed them back to me. Nothing more was said and slowly the conversations around the table resumed. I have learned from my observances of other families that children betray for the world to see, what kind of parents they have; coming to them when they need comforting and support, if their parents are loving; or shrinking away from their parents if the parents are abusive, harsh, or unloving. Abused children will out their parents at the most inopportune times, for the parents, that is.

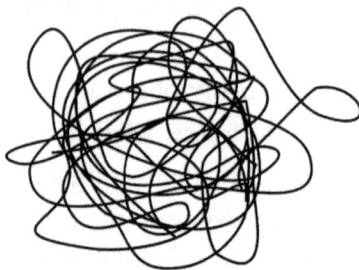

CHAPTER 24
Girls

Like any other heterosexual teenager, I had a strong attraction to girls. However, due to my mother's cruelty, I was afraid of getting into a relationship with them. My father did not help the matter. Case in point - when I was about 14, my mother said she wanted me to run down some sewing material that she had cut out from a pattern for a woman to sew together for herself. The woman lived about half a mile from our house. I reluctantly said, "okay." My mother said that it was not ready to be taken down yet and that when it was, it would be in a box on our steps going up to the second floor. One day the box appeared. I let it sit there for a few days until she started bugging me about it. The woman had a daughter my age that I did not like. In grade school she had been the teacher's pet and we had had to listen to her stories of grandeur and silly witticisms. She was very smart, but that was not why I was attracted to girls as a teenager. One afternoon, as I was about to go up to my room, there was that damn box lying on the step, so I picked it up and ran it down to the woman's house. I knocked on the door but fortunately nobody was home, so I put it inside the screen door and ran home. Sometime later that day in the afternoon, a Saturday, when my father was home and he and I were in the living room watching something on TV, my mother entered the room and said in a demanding voice, "David, where's that box?" "I took it down to the woman like you asked," I said. "You did what?" my mother screamed. "There was more to go in it. Now the woman will think I'm crazy!" I immediately thought of something quite insensitive but equally true to say, but wisely kept it to myself. I could not believe she had repeatedly bugged me to take the box when there was more to go in it, and not told me that. I did not tell her that no one had been at home and that the package was probably still in between the doors of their house and that I could go down and get it and save her from disgrace. But all was not over. My father started saying over and over again in a loud, needling chant, "David's got a girlfriend, David's got a girlfriend," for more than half an hour. Finally, the TV program was over and I left the room. In eleventh grade there was a very pretty girl in my chemistry class and we were crazy about each other. She was as high strung as I was and we talked to each other at 90 miles a minute. Many times, the teacher had to tell us to quit talking and I'm sure he would have paddled me but she was as guilty as I was and no teacher would have paddled Sue (not her real name). One time he did yell at her so sharply that I strongly suspected that he really wanted to, as she was the one who kept talking that day. I knew that if my father saw her, I would never hear the end of it, so unfortunately, I didn't date her. After the Air Force I took a large-breasted nurse I was dating home to show her where I lived, and she, my parents, and I sat around our dining room table and talked. When we left, I asked her how she thought it went. "Okay," she said, "but your father kept staring at my breasts!" I thought back to church when I was a young boy and suddenly understood why our minister called my father "Dick" all the time instead of "Rich" like everyone else.

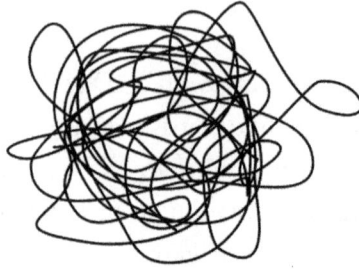

CHAPTER 25

"That's a Lazy Man's Load!"

Often, when my parents came home from food shopping, my father would order me to help carry the groceries in. This involved going down to the trunk of the car, grabbing up the old, large paper bags full of groceries, crossing the driveway, walking up the outside steps, opening first the storm door, then the kitchen door, and setting the bags of groceries onto the kitchen table or the counter. Always in a hurry to get menial chores done, I found I could line up four paper bags full of groceries in the trunk, scoop my arms under them, my upper arms holding the bags against one another, pick them up, and navigating driveway, steps, and doors, set them down in the kitchen. Every time my father saw me do it, he would scream, "That's a lazy man's load! Take two at a time!" I strongly suspected he was angry only because he couldn't do it himself on account of how fat and out of shape he was. My father would do anything he could think of that he could do better than me in such a way so that it made me feel inferior. However, whenever I could do something better than him, he found a way to be critical of it. He was simply too insecure to ever admit that I could do something better than him; so, my way became "the lazy man's load." And he would yell at me to take only two bags at a time. Of course, I never did. And in the five years I did carry four bags at a time, I never dropped or broke anything.

Another example: When it was time to turn over the dirt in our vegetable garden each spring, he would take me out in the backyard, each of us with a shovel. Knowing from experience that he would yell at me if I didn't fully sink the shovel blade into the ground to turn it over, I did so until only the handle was visible. But he yelled at me anyway. "Dig deeper," he always said. I could work nonstop until the job was done, and he couldn't, so he told me to take breaks or I'd wear myself out. I did take a break or two with him, but he never talked to me, so I went back to working straight through again, but always with his criticism for it ringing in my ears.

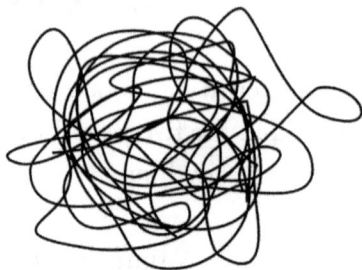

CHAPTER 26
Motorcycle Riding

My father's life growing up had not been an easy one. The third of six boys and one girl, it was my father whom his father singled out to be his gopher and workhorse. My father was the one who spaded and hoed his father's garden every year. Often, he told us the story of all the work he was made to do in it each year until I said one time, "Dad, it was your garden, not his." He reacted in an almost violent manner to this, "No, it was his garden," he roared. He also said that his oldest brother was just too smart and quick for their father to control him. That brother had owned an Indian motorcycle that my father told me about several times, and I suspected at the time that this had something to do with him forbidding me to ride motorcycles, for nothing was ever said about him not wanting me to get hurt or killed on one. However, a group of my friends had motorcycles and I sometimes rode with them.

One day at school, they told me they were going to a strip mine across town after dinner and asked if I wanted to go along. I said yes and they said they'd pick me up at seven p.m. on the street a house behind mine so that my parents wouldn't see me ride off with them. They picked me up at the designated time and we had a great time roaring along the parkway and out to the strip mine, me riding behind one of my friends. He had the nicest bike, with gold metal-flake paint and high-rise handle bars. Unfortunately, those high handle bars and me riding on the back caused him to lose control at the top of one of the strip mine hills, the handle bars twisting in his hands. As the bike was falling over, he swung his foot, encased in a heavy boot around to get off on the uphill side of the bike. The boot caught me squarely in my face rendering me helpless, and the bike fell over on top of me, pinning my left leg under the exhaust. When the bike and I finally came to a rest at the bottom of the hill, I was unable to get out from under it. He raced down and picked the bike up. I had a sizeable burn on my left calf from the muffler but was okay otherwise. When it began to get dark, we headed for home at breakneck speed. Without thinking I ran up to my house and entered the kitchen as they roared off. My mother was there and she said, "You've been riding motorcycles!" I was silent. "I just heard them roar off and your hair is standing straight up in the front. Just wait till your father gets home, are you going to get it," she said most gleefully. So used to this taunt from her, I went up to bed without thinking much about it and was soon fast asleep.

Sometime in the night I found myself being thrown out of bed and landing on the floor. Not comprehending what was happening or why, I struggled to get up only to be thrown out through the bedroom doorway and into the frame of the bathroom door which caused me to crumple onto the floor again. Still not understanding, I stood up with my back to the stairs and my father, suddenly in front of me, gave me a mighty shove down the stairs. We had railings on either side of the stairs and they, and being pushed down backwards, saved me. I was able to put my hands out and keep from bouncing down the stairs on my back by sliding down on my hands on the railings. I hit the landing, 13 stairs below with a thud, not hitting a single step. I was badly shaken but not injured. Not understanding that it would have been much safer to stay on the floor yet, I stood up as my father raced down the stairs, grabbed me and threw me into the living room where I bounced off the piano. He then threw me across the room where I landed in my mother's prize antique chair, breaking it. I fell on the floor on my back. My father jumped on top of me, grabbed my head in both of his hands and began pounding the back of my head into the floor. It wasn't long before I felt consciousness slipping away. I dully heard my mother's voice shriek, "Stop it Richard, you'll kill him!" He finally stopped and got off of me. They started arguing. "Richard, you'll kill him," she said. "I'm just trying to knock some sense into him," was his reply. She went over to her antique chair and began crying. "Oh, my beautiful chair," she sobbed. She came back to my father and they began arguing again. I got up and was standing there, feeling weak and ready to faint. I needed to go back to bed but was pretty sure if I asked to, my father would punch me full in the face. Finally, about to fall over, I risked it; "may I go to bed now?" "Go," my father roared, and I did, leaving them standing there still arguing as to whether he would have killed me or just taught me a lesson.

In a strange turn of events that can only happen to me, I rose the next morning, still in a terribly dazed and disoriented state. At breakfast my mother told me that my father had been on the famed Firestone Golf Course in Akron, Ohio the night before, playing golf in a foursome as one of the other player's guests. The man that rode over from Pittsburgh with him to also play golf, was summoned in the middle of their round by a message from his wife telling him to come home immediately, that their son had been in a terrible car accident in which the woman he rear-ended had been killed. I could just imagine what a snarly mood that had put my father in – to have his golf game interrupted while playing on one of the country's most fabulous courses. I was taking summer classes at a nearby high school as a result of my poor performance during the previous school year at the time. I went down to the bus stop after breakfast that morning, only to see the bus rounding the curve beyond me. I had missed the bus! Not wanting to go home and face the wrath of my mother, as my parents were paying for my courses, I stood at the bus stop, unsure of where to go or what to do. Down the road from my left came a motorcycle. It was the older brother of the boy whose motorcycle I had been riding on the night before. He was also going to summer school. He stopped in front of me. I did not know what to do. "Get on," he said impatiently. I looked around, and seeing no one, I got on and together we went off to summer school. Shortly before her death at age 88, long after my father had died, I told my mother about it, thinking she'd appreciate the irony of my conundrum, on that morning so long ago. She didn't. "You always were a disobedient child," she said.

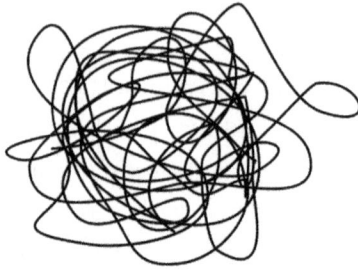

CHAPTER 27

"Listen to Her, She's Crazy"

My grandfather and I got off to a rocky start when I was born, simply because my grandmother loved me much more than she loved him. One night when I was sleeping in her bed with her (my grandfather had been sleeping in an eight-foot by five-foot windowless room for years by then), one of the slats slipped out from underneath the box springs and the mattress suddenly canted at a crazy angle. My grandmother called my grandfather to fix it. I could see he was furious with me by the angry look he sent in my direction. But after my grandmother died when I was six, a month before we moved into our new house, my grandfather and I became good friends. He was a stereo afficionado, built his own stereo amplifier, had a Gerard turntable, and expensive speakers he built the cabinets for, to get optimum sound out of them. In the 50s, he had a Hancock 750 tube tester he paid $600 for, and a Triplet volt-ohm-meter that set him back more than $100. I was fascinated by his stereo system and his test equipment. He was all too eager to teach me how to use the test equipment and at eight years of age could test almost any vacuum tube. Years later my mother told me he had tried to interest her in his stereo equipment, but that she could not be bothered.

My grandfather also had a wonderful Midwest radio. It was in a beautiful cabinet, had AM, FM, and 3 short-wave bands. The radio had 4 gang tuners which I kept very clean, and a lot of vacuum tubes. It also had a 15-inch speaker so that it had a most powerful sound. When I was 14 years old, he gave it to me. At age 16 I was in my bedroom trying to solder a new wire into it when my mother, in her bedroom across the hall, told me to take the laundry out of the hamper and down to the washing machine in the basement and wash it. I asked her if I could have a few minutes to finish what I was doing before I took the wash down. "Okay," she grudgingly replied, "just make sure you do it." The soldering was not going well and I realized I needed a knife to cut a little more insulation off of the wire. Without thinking, I ran down to the kitchen to get a knife and then ran back upstairs to my room.

"David, did you take the laundry down?" my mother yelled. "I'll do it right now," I said, knowing it was futile to try to explain what had happened. I ran to the hamper, scooped out the clothes, ran down the two flights of stairs, threw them into the washing machine, added detergent, and turned it on. As I was doing this, I could hear my mother screaming from two floors above about what a disobedient little devil I was, naming every alleged sin I had committed from the age of two. I came back up to the kitchen, got a glass of water and was standing at the sink drinking it while looking out the window when I heard heavy footsteps coming down the stairs. By this time my mother, still in her room, was up to my ninth year of sins. The footsteps crossed the dining room and came into the kitchen. Knowing it was my father, I said, "Listen to her, she's crazy." I could hear his weight shift as he stood directly behind me, then heard his shirtsleeve rustle, and knew a fist was coming my way. I juked my head to the left, an instant before his right fist shot by my head, grazing my right ear. Incensed beyond belief, I spun around and had him pinned against the refrigerator with my right hand while my left fist was cocked back higher and farther than it had ever been before. And then, I simply could not throw the punch. My father, realizing it, started throwing punches at me as hard and fast as he could. He was big and strong, but I was fast. His punches came at my head first, but I had my hands up in front of my face and none of his punches landed. He suddenly started swinging at my stomach. The first one hit me pretty hard, but then I protected my stomach and no more punches scored. I backed into a corner beside the stove and crouched down to make myself a smaller target for his fists. He changed aim again and caught me on the left cheek pretty good, but I protected my face again, and suddenly he was worn out. "Alright," I said, "I'll leave." "Go," he roared. This taught me not to voice my own opinions, no matter how accurate they were.

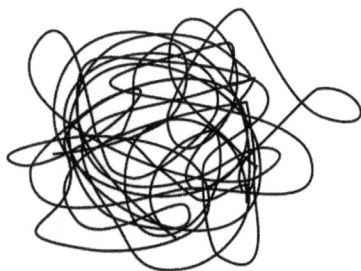

CHAPTER 28
"Now, I Want David to Answer This Question"

Right after I graduated from high school, my parents started pressuring me to go to college. I was in no hurry to go as I was working at the supermarket and really liked the people there. Somehow, they arranged an interview with the president of a highly rated private college about fifty miles away. We went for an interview and my father sat closest to the president. He was grinning as though he were going to be the student. My mother and I sat farther away with some distance between us. The president asked me a question. Knowing I was talking to a man with a PhD. in a respected position, I took a few seconds to formulate my answer. As I opened my mouth to speak, my father answered for me. The president asked me another question, and again my father answered for me. The president now said, "I want David to answer this question." After he asked it, I took a second to think and opened my mouth to respond to him, but my father again beat me to it. When we left the interview, my father said, "You dumb kid, why didn't you speak up?" I said, "You didn't give me a chance. Six years later, after my time in the

Air Force and a good semester at another school, I was accepted at that college. The same president was there still, and although some other students and I had dessert at his house one evening, our previous meeting never came up in conversation. This time, I did very well in college.

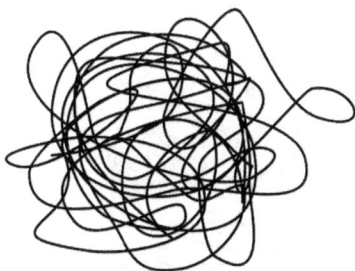

CHAPTER 29

Swings to the Head

After the incident in the kitchen in which I called my mother crazy and my father exhausted himself punching me without doing any damage, he knew that I knew his tough guy façade was a fraud. However, he must have found this too difficult to accept for he started throwing punches at my head when I wasn't looking. I was pretty sure he would land one of those haymakers one day and knock me silly. So, it was time for me to leave home. For some reason it never occurred to me to just swing back at him and inflict some real damage. I am not cruel. I wish to hurt no one, but merely to be left alone so that I can pursue my interests and enjoy my life. So, instead of beating him half to death and teaching him a lesson, I joined the Air Force and only told him about it the day before I was to leave. He came down to the car the next day and wished me well, like he really didn't want me to go and that there was nothing wrong between us.

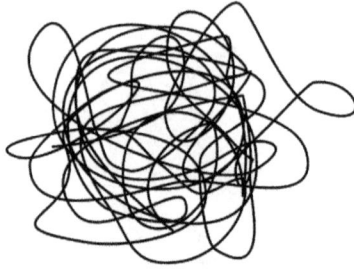

CHAPTER 30

From the Frying Pan into the Fire

In basic training I was made a squad leader the second day there. I think they chose me as one of four because I was tall, having reached my full height of just over six feet, and I appeared to be calm since I was quiet, not joking around like many of the other young men. It did not go well. My squad members would not listen to me. Because of the abuse of my father, I was not able to find the words or the authoritative manner with which to command respect.

Finally, I had had enough. I didn't need to be a leader; found telling people what to do unnatural. So, I went to one of the Training Instructors (TIs) and told him I wanted to quit. He tried to talk me out of it. I argued with him. Finally, he said to me, "You can't even keep your own shit straight." "I know that sir, that's why I want to quit," I replied, using his own words against him to strengthen my argument. It wasn't true, but it was an out and I took it. He then said to me, "You will be lucky to graduate with this flight, Airman." I did not think that could possibly be the case because I could easily do the work an airman was required to do, but I was to be taught a lesson. A day or two later, after running a mile and a half around the drill pad and being one of the first ones done, I went to my drill position and stood at ease.

An unfamiliar sergeant came up to me and told me to move up one position. "Sir," I said, "that's McClure's (not his real name) position." I knew McClure was there that day. "Airman, ten hut, forward march, one, two," he shouted at me. I was now standing in McClure's spot. Then the sergeant came around to my right side, with his chest against my arm and started screaming at me as loudly as he could, his mouth an inch from my ear. I knew it was all meant to fluster me. I had seen this done several times to other men. Finally he screamed, "Look at me Airman, look at me!" Calmly I said to him, "I can't sir." "Why not?" he yelled. "Because I am at attention, sir." Others I had previously seen in my predicament had always looked at the sergeant and received punches and kicks for their infraction of moving while at Attention. My not looking at the sergeant though, really infuriated him. He leaned harder into me and started screaming and spitting into my ear all types of abuse, calling me "dumb, dumb," as often as he could. Five minutes went by and I was really starting to get angry. I started thinking. "I know he is pressed up against my right side so that I cannot hit him, or so he thinks. I'm left-handed, something he should know since I'm wearing my watch on my right wrist and it is visible. I can easily step back quickly with my right foot and smash him in the mouth with my left fist. Or, using the same maneuver, karate chop him in his throat and try to end his life." However, going to Leavenworth for several years because of this guy simply did not seem worth it. He kept on.

When I thought I could stand it no longer, a sudden calm came over me. I began listening to his words. It became comical as I realized that this was the dumbest human being I had ever heard speak. He simply murdered the English language, not even able to put two cuss words together properly, which were 85 percent of his vocabulary.

There was a gentle breeze blowing and I began swaying ever so slightly, enjoying it, hardly hearing him. Then he startled me, "You're laughing at me boy, aren't you dumb, dumb? You're laughing at me, aren't you boy?" Unprepared for this, I felt my lips move out to laugh as I lost control of my face and I struggled mightily to bring my lips back in against my teeth. He was watching me intently and I was sure he was going to hit me, but strangely he didn't. He just redoubled his screaming until I was thinking of ending his life again. And then suddenly he quit and walked away. Watching him out of the corner of my eye, I knew he would quickly turn around and try to catch me doing something I shouldn't be doing. But I had beaten the bastard fair and square at his own game and this demanded a celebration! He did turn suddenly around as I knew he would, and as soon as he turned back around again, I extended my right arm and flipped him the bird in a grand gesture. Every one saw me do it, including the drill instructor up on the stand in front of us, leading calisthenics. After drill was over everyone rushed me, slapping me on the back and saying, "That was awesome." They too had either received abuse or witnessed other Airmen being thrashed for breaking while at Attention, and they were glad to see one of their own win this game.

But I had not learned a valuable lesson - that one must respect the rank if not the man and withstand all the abuse that was dished out, for one is the mere property of the government when in the military. Thinking all was over, I was proven wrong. The fourth squad leader now came at me with a vengeance. I strongly believed he was put up to it at the time and because of later incidents at a future base at which I served, became certain of it. When we were standing at Attention in the chow line now, he came up to me and start punching and kicking me. When I had to break from Attention in order not to lose my balance and fall over, he would scream at me, "You're at attention, get back in line," and then continue to punch and kick me.

It was a hopeless situation for me. If I hit the guy, I would go to jail. He did this twice before three other men broke from attention and rescued me. They surrounded me and started punching and kicking him, saying, "You're hurting our friend, cut it out, leave him alone." This encouraged the other men in our flight and soon 20 or more men were punching and kicking him. He stopped; he had to. And no other incidents followed this one, for all could see that any future abuse of me would lead to mass mutiny. I was Teflon now and graduated with my flight. However, I had not learned my lesson, and these incidents followed me to my permanent base.

I was assigned to RAF Lakenheath in England. After a month or two, it was announced that the wing commander, a full colonel, would inspect our barracks and us, at 5 p.m. and that we were to be ready for him. I was not looking forward to it, but was ready at the designated hour; showered, clean shaven and properly dressed, and my room was very clean and in order. Though a double-room, my barracks-mate had gotten a medical discharge shortly before. In came the wing commander at the announced hour and down the hall he came, right past my room and down to the end of the hall. As three rooms' doors were very close together there, I could hear him talking to four men at once. He was joking with them and they were laughing. After a while he came back up the hall and entered my room, passing other rooms along the way. He walked right past me to the far end of the small room and turned around to face me. He said to me, "At ease, airman," and I went from Attention to the At ease position. He asked me how I liked it there. I lied and said, "I like it fine sir." He asked me how the chow was and I lied again and said, "It's very good sir." Then he acted a little more friendly and asked me where I was from. I did not like this. I preferred to be very formal with him, but unfortunately followed his lead and got a little comfortable with him. I told him where I was from, Pittsburgh. He then asked me how I liked Pittsburgh. I proceeded to tell him some of the things I liked about my home town when he cut me off, saying sharply, "Troop, Atten hut." He walked up to me, right under my nose where I could not see him as he was only 5 feet 4 inches tall, and proceeded to tell me in a very commanding voice that he didn't give a damn about me or my hometown. Feeling very angry and abused, I answered his following questions using respectful language but in the most disrespectful tone I could manage. It did not go unnoticed and I was to pay a high price for the disrespect, for he had the authority to tell all on base how to treat me, and he fully used it to my detriment. It all culminated about two years later when I was told to report to his office one day. Once there, he told me that I had run from the police the week before and that I was no longer allowed to drive on base. The incident he referred to was a night when I was coming home from the Rod and Gun club at the far end of the base on a Friday night. It was out on a very dark and lonely road and as I was driving back to my barracks, a car came up from behind me at a very high rate of speed and started flashing its high beams at me. Not knowing who it was and also aware that there had been trouble on base, I was not about to stop; so I took off. I was in my MG and the car behind me was no match for it. I raced onto the residential part of the base, past my barracks, went out the other end of the base and then came back in another entrance, looped around the hospital, turned off my lights, did a quick left-hand turn and parked behind my barracks, then went in and up to bed.

Now, in the commander's presence, I quickly understood I had been set up. "If they were the police, why didn't they turn on their lights and siren?" I asked. "The car didn't have any," the colonel replied. I wanted to ask him how he knew that, but didn't. "Then why didn't they go past me and block the road if they wanted me to stop?" He was silent for a moment, and then he said, "I've been promoted to General." Stunned beyond belief, now fully realizing what it was all about (the Wing Commander of the base, a General now, having called me to his office about a minor traffic incident he had orchestrated, to brag to me, a 3-stripe sergeant, that he had been promoted to General!). My mouth fell open and I looked thoroughly appalled, like I truly was. Instead of saying, "Congratulations Sir," like I should have done, I found I could say nothing. Alas, I still had not learned my lesson. Though I obeyed every order I was given all three years I was at Lakenheath, and did my work diligently, my life would have been so much easier and much less painful there, if I had just respected his rank. But I simply could not respect the man, nor could I hide my disrespect. And I know I was purposely sent to the base of a 5-foot, 4-inch commander, so that I could be taught a lesson and he could have his little ego stroked.

A week later, immediately after the Pirates won the 7th game of the 1971 World Series on October 17, 1971, which I listened to on Armed Forces radio with 3 other men, they suggested that we go out driving. As it was 6 hours later in England than on the East Coast, it was about midnight in England when the game ended. I thought it strange when the other men suggested we go driving then, as they were working the day shift. I however, was working the afternoon shift, so I said okay. Two of them were rooming in the room at the far end of the hall and were some of the ones the colonel had laughed it up with two years before. They rode together in one of their MGs and I followed in mine with one of their friends from another barracks that I barely knew. They drove at a very high rate of speed along straight roads I did not know and I followed.

After quite a while they stopped, so I pulled up beside them and rolled down my window. "You lead for a while," one of them said. Immediately suspicious, I drove at a much slower speed, but it was not slow enough. Suddenly there was a hairpin turn in what had been a straight road for miles. I put my car into a four-wheel skid and was negotiating the bend nicely when a blinding light came through my passenger window. And then, a horrendous crash as my car came to an immediate halt. My passenger died that night. The man in the car that T-boned us had his legs broken. I was pretty much unhurt. It was a horrible night. "You did that on purpose," I angrily told the two other men and would have hit them but my right side had slammed into the edge of the passenger seat and I was in terrible pain. Besides this, my passenger was moaning in a deeply mournful way that I had never heard before and I knew that he needed immediate attention. I never did confront the men who set me up. And ironically, the wing commander did not call me back into his office. Though knowing I had been set up, my mind took full responsibility for the accident and I felt terrible about it for years. It was to cause me to make some very bad decisions in the future.

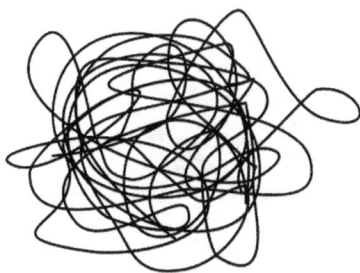

CHAPTER 31

Hang Up, You're Wasting My Money

Shortly after my accident I called my father to talk to him about it; I suppose to get a little sympathy and support. There was no other way to call him than collect, so I did. I could hear him reluctantly accept the charges. When I told him the story of my accident, he said, sharply, "Why are you calling me about it? Hang up, you're wasting my money." I tried again to tell him, not willing to give up. "What do you want me to do about it?" he said, "you're wasting my money, hang up the phone." After several more times of telling me to hang up, he hung up, himself. I just sat there for a few moments, holding the receiver in my hand. It's the loneliest I have ever felt.

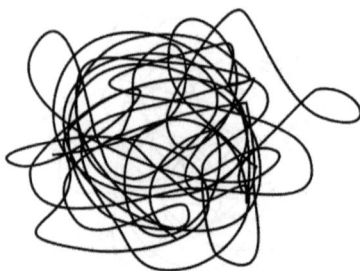

CHAPTER 32
"Hit Me, Hit Me"

After being honorably discharged from the Air Force, I went home to live with my parents again before going off to college. My father was a completely different man, having gotten a great job as an independent rep of a large international corporation and consequently making lots of money. He called on the heads in a certain department of all the major international corporations in Pittsburgh and the larger tri-state area. Somehow, he was good at wining and dining them. He became quite friendly with two men in particular, paying for their many meals, even more drinks, and their golf games. Money was no object now, but he often came home drunk, late at night. One late morning, my mother asked me to go into town to pick my father up at a certain bar. He had gone into town with another man that morning and needed a ride home. An hour later, I entered the bar at 12:00 p.m. and there was my father, drunk as a skunk, at the bar. I was repulsed at the sight of him. However, I sat beside him and ordered a drink. We got into a conversation and were soon arguing.

"All you think about is money," I remember saying to him. I did not bring up the incident of him telling me to hang up the phone when I called him after my accident, but I'm pretty sure it was on my mind.

Somehow the conversation got around to him saying to me, "Well hit me then, hit me." The third time he said it, I did – a round house left hook right to his face. The bartender bellowed, "Cut it out or leave!" Stunned, my father wobbled on his bar stool, saying, "You hurt me, you really hurt me." Actually, sitting on the bar stool didn't allow me to get my legs into the punch so it really wasn't that hard of a hit. He tried to order another drink but I waved the bartender off. "It's time to go," I said. He didn't want to leave, but forcing him to his feet, I twisted his left arm behind his back and marched him out of the bar and to the car. He struggled to get free, but I had been running six miles a day in just over 31 minutes and exercising my upper body for two years, so I was much stronger than him. We rode home in silence. We walked through the door into the dining room, and there was my mother looking at him in disgust. I bent over the dining room table to continue working on something I had been doing before I left to go get him. Suddenly he had his arms around my back and got his body beneath me so that my back had to support his two hundred thirty pounds. As he hung there, he kept jerking as hard as he could, trying to break my back. I couldn't go down to the floor on top of him because I was above the table, leaning over it, and he was below the table. It was quite a strain, but my back held and I was finally able to wrestle him off of me. Years later, when he was in the hospital dying of cancer, I apologized for hitting him. "Oh well," he said, "I probably deserved it."

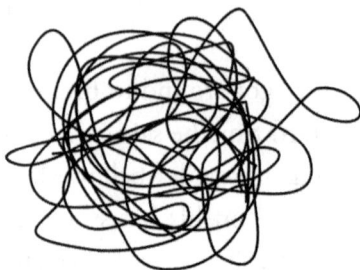

CHAPTER 33
Kids on Weekends

We were living in Akron at the time my wife and I separated. She took our children with her back to Pittsburgh. Determined to keep a relationship with them going, I asked my parents if I could bring my children to their home for a weekend a month as they lived about an hour away from my wife. They said yes. So, I drove to Pittsburgh on a late Friday afternoon after work, picked up my two children, and went to my parent's home. My children and I had a good time, but toward the end of it my mother told me my father had said to her, "What does he want to play with those children for?" After taking my children home to their mother, I stopped at my parents' home again as it was on the way back to Akron. They both confronted me. "You can't bring your children here anymore. It disrupts our lives too much," they said. I was stunned. I had done everything for my children when at my parent's home. All my parents did was see them and, I guess, hear them. For six years after that, I drove from Akron to Pittsburgh and back to Akron on Friday evenings, once or twice a month, (about three hours in each direction as my ex-wife lived on the south side of town). Though we had some great conversations on our rides to Akron, the trips back to Pittsburgh were always in silence. It was hard on all three of us.

One time I picked up only my son for a weekend and for some reason stopped at my parent's home on the way back to Akron. I had just bought a little Oldsmobile Cutlass Calais. It was a pretty car, burgundy, with matching velour bucket seats. As a child, whenever my father and I went somewhere in the car, he would always tell me to get in on the driver's side and crawl across the seat to the passenger side. Without fail, as I did so he would say, "Keep your feet off the seat," and give me a hard whack on my bottom. It had just rained when I had my son there, but I said to him, "Just get in on my side and crawl across the seat." I watched with satisfaction as his shoes dripped water on my nice velour seat. I thought this would teach my father something, but I got more than I expected. He suddenly rushed toward my car to give my son a whack. I quickly stepped in front of him and snarled, "Don't you dare touch my son!" It stopped him cold. It was the first time I saw the great difference in size between him and a five-year-old, like I was when he was beating on me. It both shocked me and made me very angry.

Another time, I had my children at my apartment in Akron and when I came into the living room from my bedroom, there was my son, lying on the sofa, fast asleep, with his feet on the cushion. Growing up, my father had forbidden us from lying on the sofa and when he caught us doing it, even though our shoes were off, we received a whack and a reprimand. This despite the fact that he did it regularly, his shoes on or off. He also forbade us from eating in the living room, and he did this regularly also, lying on the sofa, his feet on the cushion, eating an apple while watching golf matches. When I saw my son lying there, an overwhelming impulse rose up from somewhere within me to walk over and swipe his feet off the sofa. As I walked over to do so, he opened his eyes, looked up at me, smiled, closed his eyes, and went back to sleep. It melted my heart instantly and he could have spilled a gallon of chocolate milk on the sofa with his feet on it then, and I wouldn't have cared a bit. I was and am, so very thankful he looked up at me and smiled when he did.

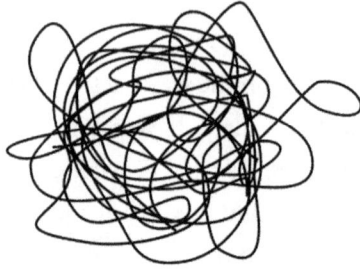

In Conclusion

I hope you have found this book easy to read. But, as I said at the beginning, I wrote it to send a message about the harm that child abuse does, for it alters one's thinking the entire course of his or her life and so adversely affects the quality of it. It prevents him from reaching anything near his real potential, makes him think he is not good enough, and robs him of happiness.

My father was the son of a minister, so you would have expected him to be a kind, gentle man. However, his father was violent, and rather than putting the fear of God in my father, he put the fear of man in him instead. (To his dying day, my father insisted that his father was one of the strongest men that ever lived.) My father acted tough but as I grew up, I learned that he was a very fearful, angry man. His father had turned him into a violent man like himself, often mean and nasty to his own children, to cover up his weakness and insecurities. Amazingly, almost to his day of death, my father insisted he could beat me up, even though he could barely breathe. It made no sense, but that is what abuse does to a person.

Throughout his life, my father almost never laughed or smiled. He did not have a sense of humor, and so, never talked in a humorous way. His words to us, his children, were so very often just pithy slogans. Among his favorites were:

> *I only owe you a roof over your head and three squares (meals) a day.*
> *You're crying with a loaf of bread under your arm.*
> *You've got the world by the tail on a downhill pull.*
> *Spare the rod and spoil the child.*
> *Children should be seen and not heard.*
> *The will of the child must be broken.*
> *You don't know how easy you have it.*
> *You think money grows on trees.*
> *You're going to break your arm, patting yourself on the back.*

My father led a joyless life. Though a sixth grade Sunday school teacher for many years, he was unable to talk to us in a calm, peaceful manner in words that were his own. He had no substance. How sad that his father, a minister, raised him in this fashion.

Fearful, angry men often treat their children the same way their fathers treated them. The sad truth is that child abuse is so destructive and painful that the abused child is unable to comprehend what is happening to him, how it feels, or what it means, for this is the only way he can survive. The abused person has no real sense of self, for abuse is so vile that its victims must split themselves off from the suffering child and look at him or her as though they are another. In this sense, the victims of abuse are not aware that they are being abused. His or her mind and body just absorb the abuse and store it up. It usually registers, emotionally, as fear and rage in one's subconscious and even deeper, to adversely affect one's mood, outlook, temperament, and behavior in later years. I was in therapy for more than a year before I realized that I had been severely abused throughout my childhood. Then came the anger and the rage and all the pent-up emotions.

I thank God that for some reason I did not abuse my children. I always sought to do what was best for them, wanting to protect them, and to see them do well, being happy, and enjoying life. How this happened I do not know. I never had the thought that I did not want to do to them what my father, and my mother, did to me. I just naturally loved them from the moment they were born. I truly thank God for that and include them and my grandchildren in my prayers every morning and night.

After my father died of cancer at age sixty-four, and was buried, I was drawn to his grave-sight and would drive there and sit in my car, looking at his tombstone, wistfully wishing that it had been much different between us. After several times of doing this, my wishful thinking was over. I moved on and never again visited his grave.

I implore all parents to treat their children with love, patience, and care. Recognize how small they are compared to your much larger size, and remember it is from you that they receive their understanding of themselves, other people, and the world. You don't have to be very intelligent; you don't need to be educated. All you need do is love and accept them, and show them that you do. They will be much happier, healthier individuals because of it. Show them they are your number one priority!